To

Owen

From

Charlie

We can do no great things,
Only small things with great love.

Mother Teresa of Calcutta

The prayers and illustrations in this book were
selected from *The Lion Treasury of Children's Prayers*,
published by Lion Publishing in 1999
Illustrations copyright © 1999 Alison Jay
Original edition published in English under the title
Prayers for a Special Child by Lion Publishing plc,
Oxford, England. Copyright © 2001 Lion
Publishing plc.

North American Edition published by Good Books,
2002. All rights reserved.

PRAYERS FOR A TREASURED CHILD
Copyright © 2002 by Good Books, Intercourse, PA 17534
International Standard Book Number: 1-56148-348-6

Acknowledgments
Every effort has been made to trace and contact
copyright owners. We apologize for any inadvertent
omissions or errors.

"The angels love you" by Sophie Piper copyright
© Lion Publishing. "Jesus keep us safe today" by
Joan Gale Thomas from *Our Father*, published by A.R.
Mowbray & Co. Reprinted by permission of Deborah
Sheppard. "Let our friendships be strong, O Lord"
by Christopher Herbert from *The Prayer Garden – An
Anthology of Children's Prayers*, compiled
by Christopher Herbert, published by HarperCollins
Publishers Ltd. Reprinted by permission. "Bless all
the homeless ones" by Dorothy E. Baker from *Praise
Him*, compiled by
M. Grace Bartlett, published in 1959 by the
Church Information Office.

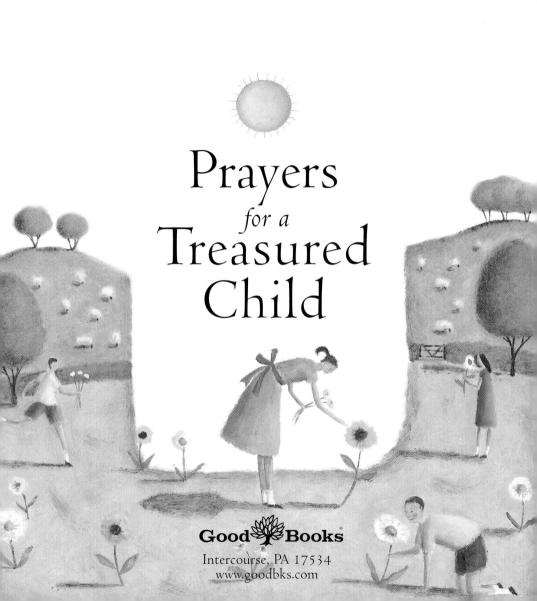

Prayers
for a
Treasured
Child

Good Books

Intercourse, PA 17534
www.goodbks.com

Thank you, God in heaven,
For a day begun.
Thank you for the breezes,
Thank you for the sun.
For this time of gladness,
For our work and play,
Thank you, God in heaven,
For another day.

Traditional

Jesus keep us
Safe today,
And keep all evil
Far away.

Watch my feet
In case I fall –
Let nothing frighten
Me at all,

And let my guardian
Angel be
Walking hand in hand
With me.

Joan Gale Thomas

God bless the field and bless the furrow
Stream and branch and rabbit burrow...
Bless the minnow, bless the whale,
Bless the rainbow and the hail,
Bless the nest and bless the leaf,
Bless the righteous and the thief,

Bless the wing and bless the fin,
Bless the air I travel in,
Bless the mill and bless the mouse,
Bless the miller's bricken house,
Bless the earth and bless the sea,
God bless you and God bless me.

Anonymous

He prayeth best,
  Who loveth best
All things both great and small;
For the dear God
  Who loveth us,
He made and loveth all.

Samuel Taylor Coleridge (1772–1834)

Dear God,
Be good to me,
The sea is so wide
And my boat is so small.

Prayer of Breton fishermen

Bless this house which is our home
May we welcome all who come.

Anonymous

Let our friendships be strong, O Lord,
that they become a blessing to others…
Let our friendships be open, O Lord,
that they may be a haven for others…
Let our friendships be gentle, O Lord,
that they may bring peace to others…
for Jesus' sake. Amen.

Christopher Herbert

Johnny Appleseed Grace

The Lord is good to me,
And so I thank the Lord
For giving me the things I need,
The sun, the rain, the appleseed.
The Lord is good to me.

Attributed to John Chapman, American pioneer
and planter of orchards (1774–1845)

Bless all the homeless ones
Near and far away,
And all the sad and lonely ones
Day by day.

And help us to remember them
Always in prayer,
And leave them, heavenly Father,
In your care.

Dorothy E. Baker

Dear Jesus, as a hen covers her chicks with her wings to keep them safe, protect us this dark night under your golden wings.

Prayer from India

Peace of the running waves to you,
Deep peace of the flowing air to you,
Deep peace of the quiet earth to you,
Deep peace of the shining stars to you,
Deep peace of the shades of night to you,
Moon and stars always giving light to you,
Deep peace of Christ, the Son of Peace, to you.

Traditional Gaelic blessing

Day is done,
Gone the sun
From the lake,
From the hills,
From the sky.
Safely rest,
All is well!
God is nigh.

Anonymous